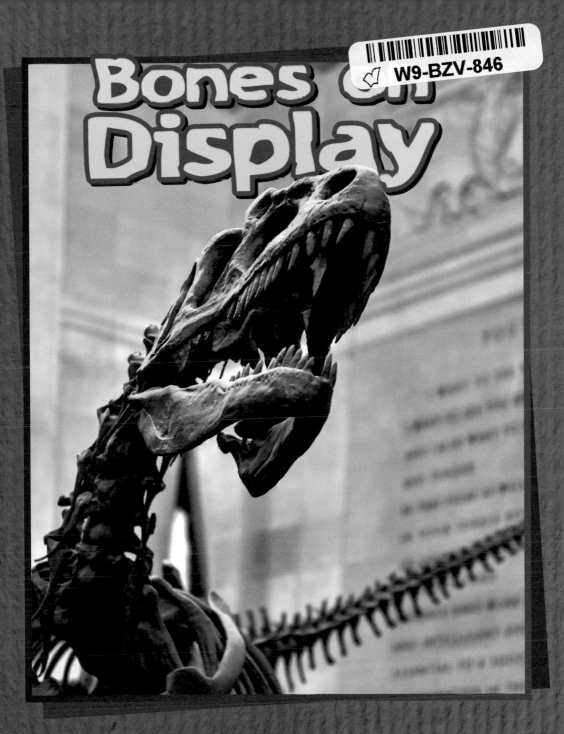

Bones on Display

Elisa Jordan, M.A.

Contributing Author

Jennifer Lawson

Consultants

Dr. Don E. Wilson
Emeritus Curator, Zoologist
National Museum of Natural History

Sharon Banks
3rd Grade Teacher
Duncan Public Schools

Publishing Credits

Rachelle Cracchiolo, M.S.Ed., *Publisher*

Conni Medina, M.A.Ed., *Managing Editor*

Diana Kenney, M.A.Ed., NBCT, *Content Director*

Véronique Bos, *Creative Director*

Robin Erickson, *Art Director*

Michelle Jovin, M.A., *Associate Editor*

Mindy Duits, *Senior Graphic Designer*

Smithsonian Science Education Center

Image Credits: p.6, p.7 (top), p.8, pp.8–9, p.11 (bottom), p.12 (bottom), pp.14–15, p.18 (bottom), p.19 (top), p.24 © Smithsonian; p.14 (bottom) © Field Museum, photo by Kate Golembiewski; p.21 Axel Mauruszat; p.25 Zuma Press/Alamy; pp.26–27 PA Images/Alamy; all other images from iStock and/or Shutterstock.

Library of Congress Cataloging-in-Publication Data

Names: Jordan, Elisa, author.
Title: Bones on display / Elisa Jordan.
Description: Huntington Beach, CA : Teacher Created Materials, [2019] | Audience: K to Grade 3. | Includes index. |
Identifiers: LCCN 2018030202 (print) | LCCN 2018036677 (ebook) | ISBN 9781493869022 | ISBN 9781493866625
Subjects: LCSH: Paleontology--Juvenile literature. | Bones--Exhibitions--Juvenile literature.
Classification: LCC QE714.5 (ebook) | LCC QE714.5 .J67 2019 (print) | DDC 560--dc23
LC record available at https://lccn.loc.gov/2018030202

Teacher Created Materials

5301 Oceanus Drive
Huntington Beach, CA 92649-1030
www.tcmpub.com
ISBN 978-1-4938-6662-5
© 2019 Teacher Created Materials, Inc.
Printed in Malaysia
Thumbprints.21251

Table of Contents

Where Bones Live

What if skeletons could talk? They can! Well, they can sort of talk to you. You might think that's a little strange, but it is true. Every bone has a story. People just have to learn how to read bones' stories.

Bones can tell you where animals lived or what they ate. They can also tell you when they lived. Some bones date back millions of years! That means we can learn about real animals from long, long ago. You can find these bones at natural history museums. This kind of museum helps people learn about life on Earth.

This *Tyrannosaurus rex* (*T. rex*) is on display at the Hong Kong Science Museum.

This *Stegosaurus* is on display at the Natural History Museum in London.

This *Triceratops* skull is on display outside Smithsonian's natural history museum in Washington, DC.

The Smithsonian Institution has a well-known natural history museum. It is called the National Museum of Natural History. It is huge! People can learn a lot of things there. They can see bones, plants, and rocks from the past.

The museum is more than a hundred years old. It has grown a lot through the years. Some **exhibits** have changed. But the purpose has stayed the same. Museum workers hope to teach people about the world. They do this by teaching people about the past.

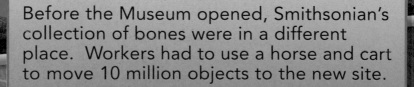

Before the Museum opened, Smithsonian's collection of bones were in a different place. Workers had to use a horse and cart to move 10 million objects to the new site.

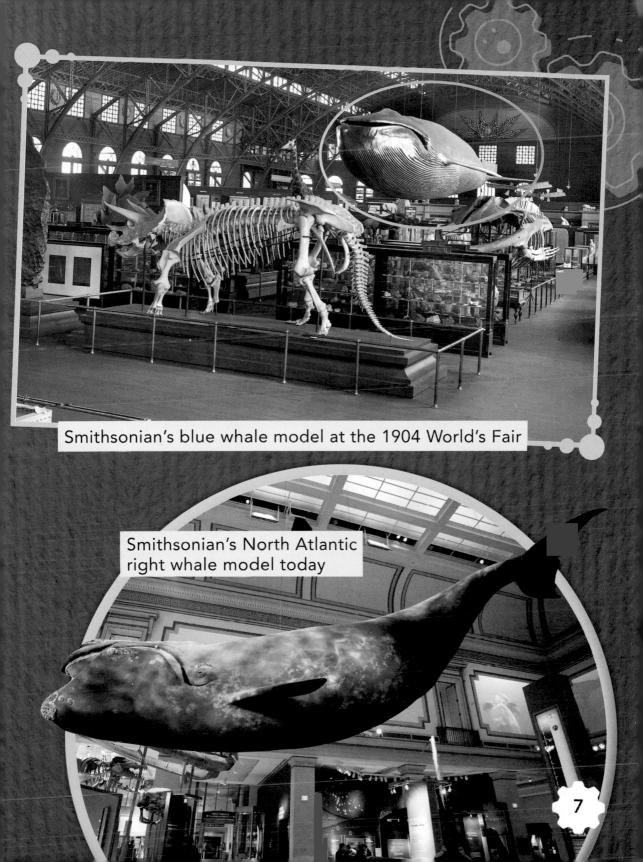

Smithsonian's blue whale model at the 1904 World's Fair

Smithsonian's North Atlantic right whale model today

Smithsonian set up a special exhibit for bones. Workers were not sure that anyone would want to come. But they did! Big crowds went to see the bone displays—especially people who lived nearby.

Soon, exhibits opened in new places around the world. More and more people could see these bones from the past. Now, these exhibits are easy to find. People can visit museums to learn about animals and people from the past.

Stegosaurus display in Smithsonian's National Museum of Natural History in the 1950s

Smithsonian's early Bone Hall

Smithsonian's bone collection was on display in this building until 1910.

Who, What, Where

A lot of people visit museums. A lot of people work at museums too. Many workers are out where people can see them. They may tell people about exhibits. Or, they may keep exhibits clean.

People do not see all museum workers though. Scientists work behind the scenes. Sometimes, they need quiet places to work. They study things, such as art or bones. Other times, they may search for bones to add to exhibits. This part of their job is called **fieldwork**. Once they are done with fieldwork, they bring bones back to their museums.

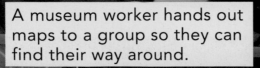

A museum worker hands out maps to a group so they can find their way around.

Scientists search for bones.

Scientists wrap bones to send to the National Museum of Natural History.

After bones are collected, scientists have to take care of them. Bones can be very old. That means people have to be careful when they work with them. When bones first come to a museum, workers clean them. They use many tools to chip away dirt and soil without harming the bones.

Once bones are clean, workers have to put them back together. Over time, bones can break into pieces. Workers have to glue all the pieces back together. Sometimes, the pieces are very small! It can be hard work.

A scientist unwraps bones at the National Museum of Natural History.

A scientist uses an air scribe to chip away dirt.

Technology & Engineering

Tools of the Trade

Scientists use many tools to clean bones. Sometimes, they use air scribes. These tools are like tiny jackhammers. Other times, they use picks or brushes.

Once the glue has dried, workers make **casts**, or copies, of the bones. Workers display these copies to keep real bones safe. First, a worker must make a mold. To do so, the worker places a bone on a clay bed. Next, they paint the bone with liquid rubber. Once the rubber is dry and has hardened, the worker pulls it off. This leaves a mold of half the bone. Then, the worker flips the bone and makes a mold of the other half.

Workers then put both halves of the mold together. They pour plastic or **resin** into the mold and wait. Once the liquid is dry, workers separate the mold. They are left with an exact copy of the bone.

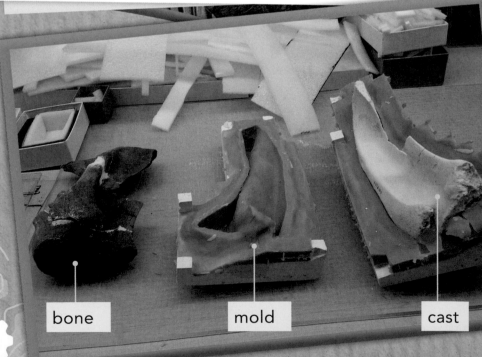

bone   mold   cast

This is a cast of a dinosaur skull.

This *T. rex* skull cast has been painted and displayed.

Painting Bones

A cast of a bone is white. But most museums have bones that are very old. These bones are usually more brown than white. So, artists paint the casts. Artists use different shades to make the copies look real.

15

Once casts have been made, scientists can study them. They might compare the shapes and sizes to other animals. They might try to learn about the animals and their **habitats**. They might look at teeth. Teeth tell them which foods animals ate. Scientists might check for wings or fins. Wings mean an animal might have flown. Fins mean it might have swam.

Scientists become experts on **fossils**. They share what they learn. They share with scientists who are near and far. Each animal is different, so that means there are lots of fossils to study!

The Truth about Teeth

Teeth and bones are both made of **minerals**. But, teeth are stronger than bones. If a person breaks a bone, it can regrow. But if a person breaks a tooth, it cannot regrow.

T. rex tooth

This bird fossil has wings scientists can study.

Plesiosaurus tooth

Mosasaurus tooth

Megalodon tooth

On Display

Some bone casts are used to make skeletons for exhibits. They help people "see" the past.

The first step in making this type of display is design. Museum workers want to set bones a certain way. They might make a bird's skeleton look like it is flying. Or, workers might make a fish's bones look like it's swimming. Huge skeletons might be placed next to small ones. The difference in size can shock people. Exhibits help people picture what animals might have looked like when they were alive.

This *Basilosaurus* is on display at Smithsonian's National Museum of Natural History in 1912.

In 1989, workers redesigned the *Basilosaurus* to make it look like it was swimming.

The largest land animal today is the African elephant. The largest dinosaur could have weighed as much as 16 African elephants!

Once displays are designed, it is time to build them. Some skeletons are huge. The tallest dinosaur was more than 18 meters (59 feet) tall. That means museums need a lot of space to show them. Skeletons are often shown standing. That helps people see how big or small the animals were.

Living animals have **ligaments** and **tendons** that hold bones in place. But fossils do not have these because they rot away. So, workers have to build frames to hold casts. They build frames by joining metal pieces. Then, they use wires to tie the casts to the frames. Then, people can see full skeletons.

These foot bone casts are held together by wires.

Measuring Bones

When building exhibits, designers have to know how big a final skeleton will be. They have to measure the bones. Then, they have to add the measurements. That helps them find a space that is the right size.

This display is of *Giraffatitan*—one of the tallest dinosaurs that ever lived.

So Lifelike

People can learn a lot from looking at bones. But it is also fun to see what animals looked like when they were alive. Did they have spikes? Did they have fur? What color were they? This is when museums can get creative.

Museums can help guests picture what animals might have sounded or looked like when they were alive. People might hear a loud T. rex roar! Or they might see a shark swim past. Museums can also show animations of animals moving. These exhibits help people learn even more about the animals.

This computer drawing of a dinosaur shows people what it might have looked like.

People can walk around these dinosaur models at the interactive Jurassic Park in Poland.

This display shows a dinosaur hatching from an egg.

Smithsonian's National Museum of Natural History has an app for people to use. Skin and Bones brings bones to life! People can open the app and point their phones or tablets at bone displays. It shows them what animals looked like. People can even move around to see animals move with them!

People can play games on the app too. They can hear noises and guess which animals made the sounds. Or, they can "meet" scientists who work with the bones. If people live far away, they can still use the app. They can scan images at home! Apps such as Skin and Bones are a new way to learn about the past.

A museum guest uses the Skin and Bones app.

A woman uses a tablet to learn more about dinosaurs.

Listen Up

People can learn a lot from bone displays and exhibits. People have learned what Earth was like a long time ago. Bones teach people about life. They teach people about habitats too.

That is why scientists who study bones have such an important job. They can teach people about the past. When people look at bones on display, they can learn more. All they have to do is listen to the stories bones are telling.

A scientist studies a *Diplodocus* skeleton in London.

A student studies a fossil in a natural history museum.

STEAM CHALLENGE

Define the Problem

Workers at a natural history museum near your home have found a new skeleton fossil. They want to put the bones on display. They have asked you to make a model of the exhibit.

Constraints: You may only use a shoebox, clay, pipe cleaners, glue, tape, paint, colored pencils, or markers to build your exhibit.

Criteria: Your exhibit must have a skeleton of an animal and its habitat. The skeleton must be standing. You must include a few sentences to teach people about your animal.

Research and Brainstorm

Why should museum workers know how to display bones? How do exhibits help people learn about animals? How do museums make learning fun?

Design and Build

Sketch a model of your display. What purpose will each part serve? What materials will you use? Build the model.

Test and Improve

Show your model to your friends. Can they tell what your animal is? Can your model stand on its own? How can you improve it? Improve your design and try again.

Reflect and Share

What was difficult about this challenge? What did you learn? How could you add technology to help people imagine what your animal looked or sounded like?

Glossary

casts—copies made by pouring or pressing things into molds

exhibits—objects or collections that have been put out for people to view

fieldwork—work done by going out and gathering information

fossils—things, such as skeletons, that are from animals or plants that lived long ago

habitats—the types of places where animals or plants naturally live and grow

ligaments—tough pieces of tissue that keep bones and organs in place

minerals—substances that naturally form in the earth

resin—a liquid that can be made or can be taken from trees and is used to make plastics

tendons—tough pieces of tissue that connect muscles to bones

Index

Career Advice
from Smithsonian

Do you want to study bones?
Here are some tips to get you started.

"If you want to learn about animals, go outside! Then, when you are older, study biology and paleontology."
—*Don E. Wilson, Curator Emeritus*

"I find fossils that have been buried for millions of years. If you want to experience this feeling, read books about fossils. Visit museums and ask questions too!" —*Matthew T. Miller, Museum Technician*